Letts

You think *you* have a long journey to school? Meet the Alien Club, a group of jolly aliens from the planet Dunk. They all entered a competition and won first prize – to go to school on planet Earth, six thousand light years away! Lucky their space-mobile runs on recycled rubbish and can travel a hundred light years in a heartbeat!

Meet **Nok**, who finds football much easier than school, but tries all the same!

Twinx, who loves ribbons, dancing and her toy friend Mini T.

Bouncing **Pogo**, who just can't stand still!

Pogo's pet dog, the rather less lively **Zen**, who won't get out of bed for less than a Z cookie or two.

Zara P, zip zip zipping around on her scooter and making notes on everything she sees.

And **Zing**, who loves his music most of all, but thinks school is pretty cool too!

Now the Alien Club want to pass on everything they've learnt to you. All you have to do is work your way through these tests and not only will you be the cleverest Earthling around, you'll become a member of the Alien Club too! Out of this world!!!

English 10–11

Alison Head

TEST 1

Connectives

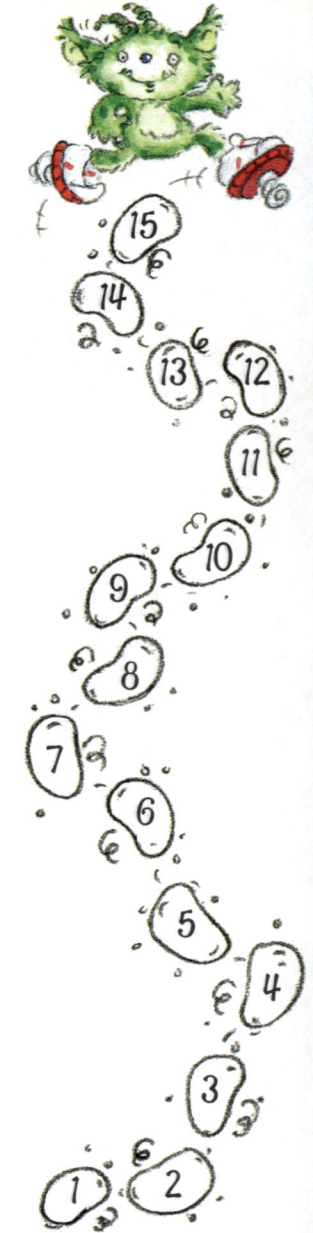

Boing, boing, boing!
I'm Pogo and I love to bounce! Too many short bounces make me dizzy, so I try to do long ones instead. It's the same with sentences. Too many short sentences can make reading hard work, so you can use **connective** words or phrases to link them.
It was late. I went to bed.
It was late **so** I went to bed.
You can also use them to link separate sentences or paragraphs together.

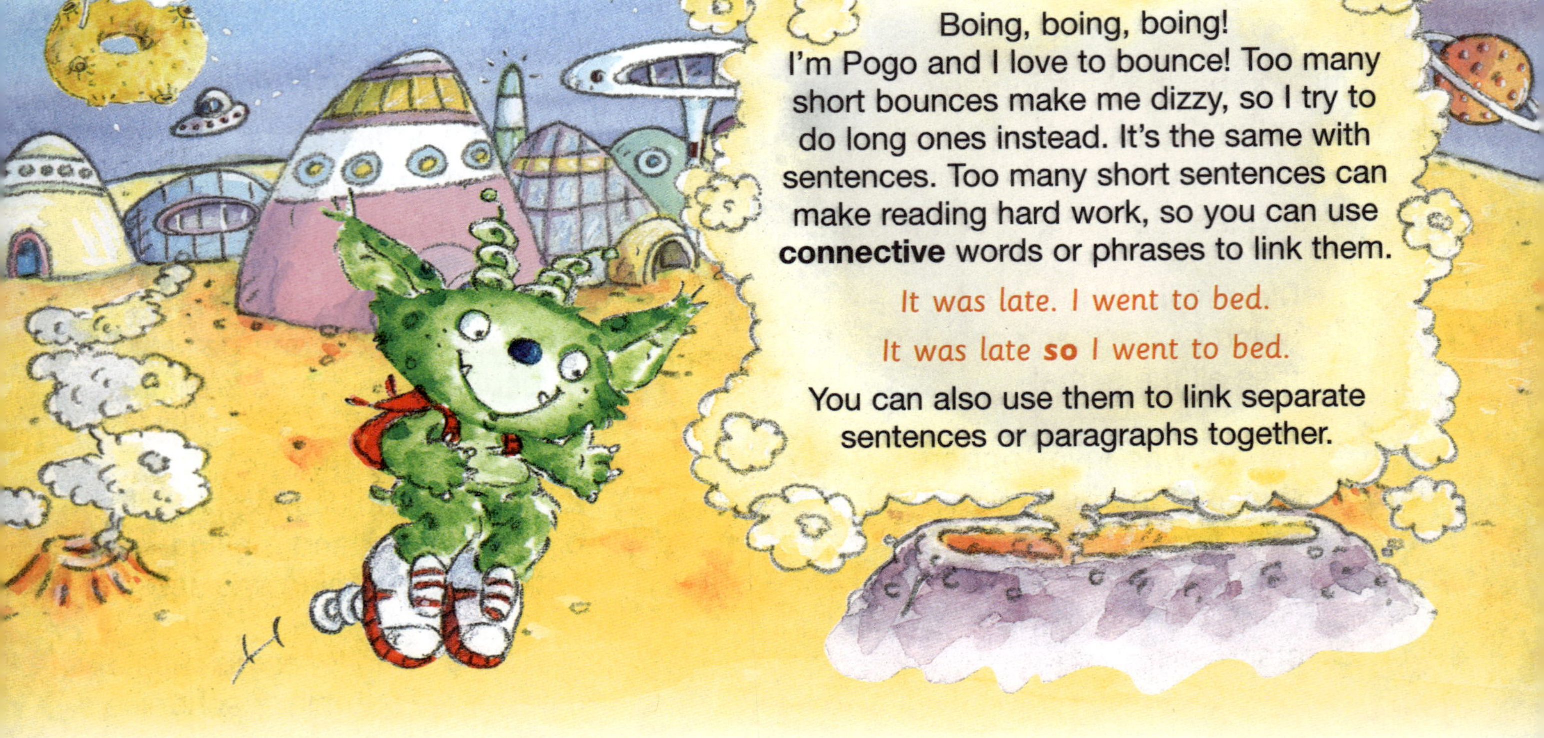

Underline the connective words or phrases in these sentences.

1 Twinx practised her ballet, so she would improve.

2 Zen was tired, but even so, he managed to eat his Z cookies.

3 Nok cleaned his boots after he had played football.

4 The space-mobile headed for Earth, then turned and came back.

5 Zara P wobbled on her jet-scooter, but she didn't fall off.

6 Zing's music was so loud that he didn't hear Zen barking.

7 Pogo has to put his springy trainers on before he can bounce.

8 Nok looked confused, as he usually did!

9 Zara P went out on her jet-scooter, despite the rain.

10 Zen kept eating until his bowl was empty.

11 The aliens won a competition and the prize was a trip to Earth.

12 Zara P made a note in her notebook, then she put it away.

13 The crater was enormous, but Pogo bounced right across it.

14 You could see the comet without a telescope, because it was so big.

15 Pogo was about to bounce, when his springs fell off.

15
14
13
12
11
10
9
8
7
6
5
4
3
2
1

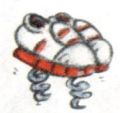

Put a spring in your step! Have a springy sticker for your certificate at the back of the book.

Colour in your score.

Changing language

Hey there! My name's Zing – music's my thing. I've been listening to the music that my mum and dad used to listen to. It's so different from the music I like.

Language changes over time too. Words go out of use and new words arrive. Most people don't use old words any more, because they sound odd in modern writing, but they can be useful if you're writing a story set in the past.

thy = your

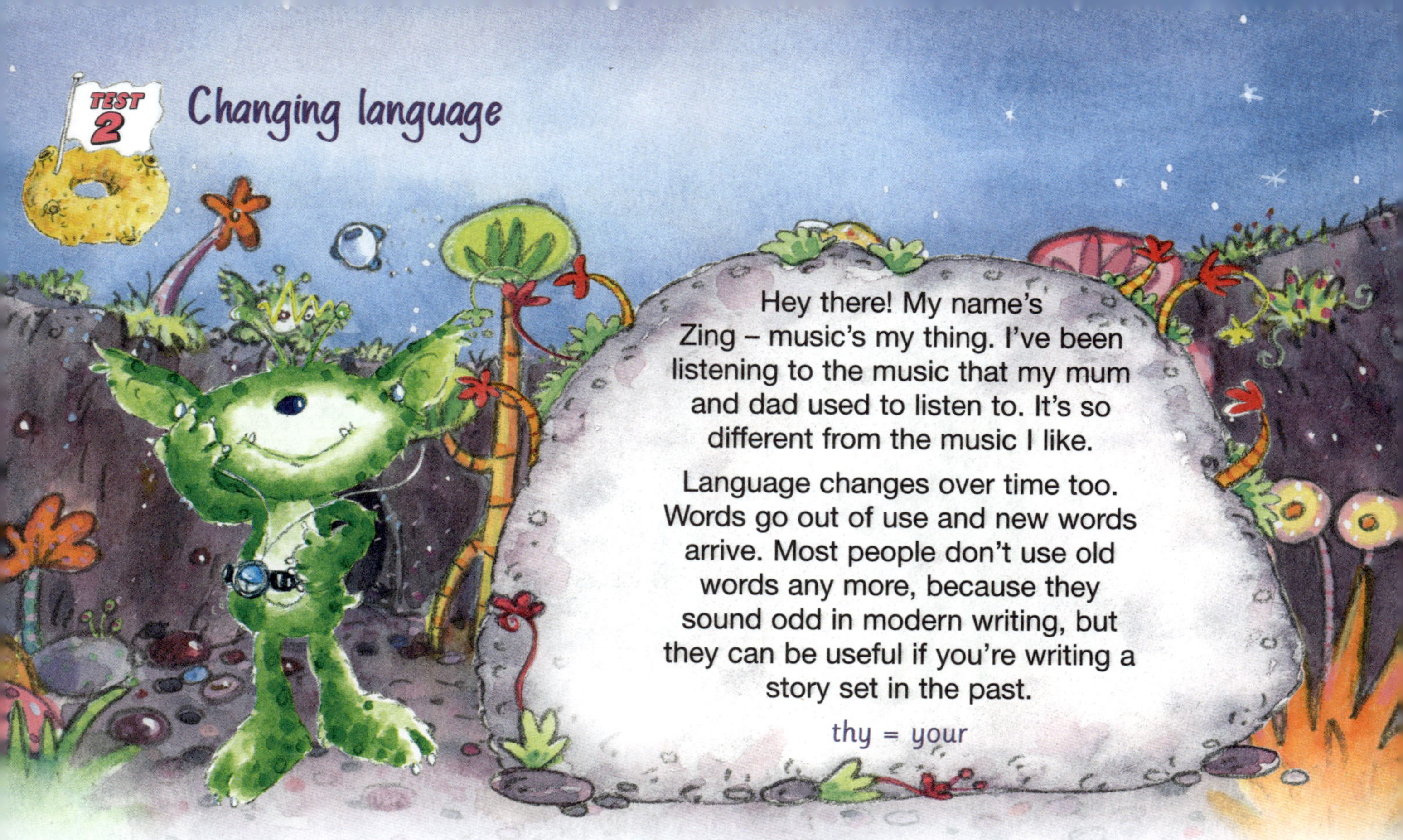

Sort these words into old and new, then write them in the correct box.

1 alas

2 email

3 forsooth

4 smoothie

5 podcast

6 shilling

7 snowboard

8 texting

9 yonder

10 serf

11 galoshes

12 solar panel

13 hither

14 website

15 squire

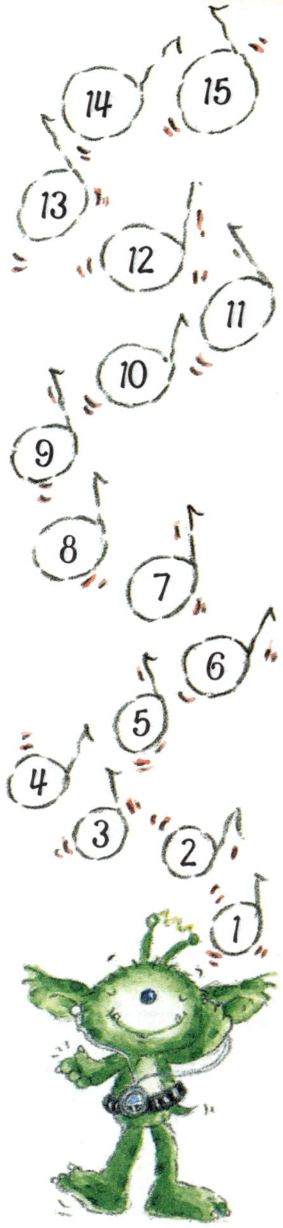

Old

_____
_____
_____
_____
_____
_____
_____

New

_____
_____
_____
_____
_____
_____
_____

Easy! Have a musical sticker for your certificate at the back of the book.

Colour in your score.

TEST 3

Active and passive verbs

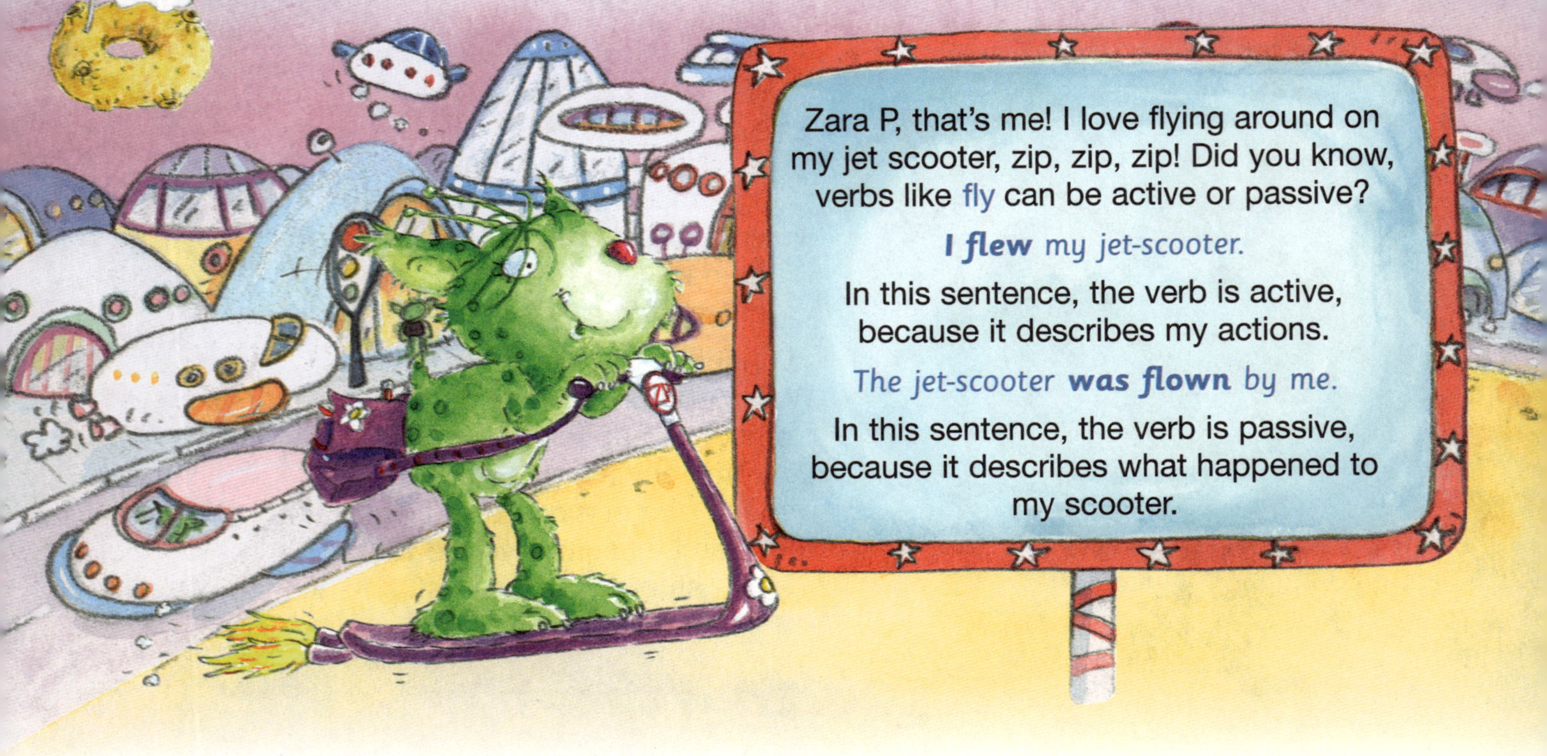

Zara P, that's me! I love flying around on my jet scooter, zip, zip, zip! Did you know, verbs like fly can be active or passive?
I flew my jet-scooter.
In this sentence, the verb is active, because it describes my actions.
The jet-scooter **was flown** by me.
In this sentence, the verb is passive, because it describes what happened to my scooter.

These sentences all use passive verbs. Write them again, with active verbs.

1 The Z cookies were eaten by Zen. ____________________

2 The space-mobile was flown by an alien.

____

3 A goal was scored by Nok. ____________________

4 A dance was performed by Twinx. ____________________

5 The music was turned up by Zing. ____________________

6 The notebook is owned by Zara P. ____________________

7 The vase was broken by Pogo. ____________________

8 Mini T was held by Twinx. ____________________

9 The competition was won by the aliens.

____

10 The scooter was fixed by Zara P. ____________________

11 A noise was made by Zen. ____________________

12 The rucksack was dropped by Pogo. ____________________

13 The space-mobile was boarded by the aliens.

____

14 The crater was played in by Pogo. ____________________

15 The trainers were put on by Zing. ____________________

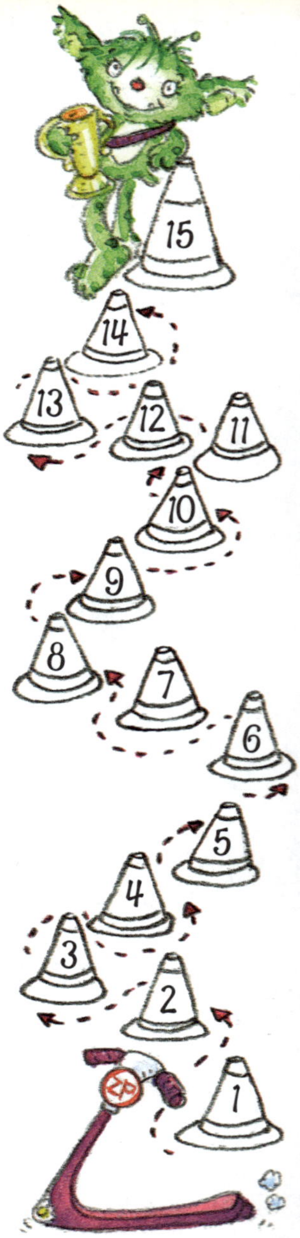

15
14
13
12
11
10
9
8
7
6
5
4
3
2
1

Colour in your score.

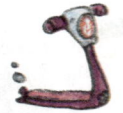

You're zippy! Have a scooter sticker for your certificate.

Hello! I'm Twinx and this is my toy friend Mini T. I'm reading Mini T a story.

The **narrator** in a story is the person who tells the story. Sometimes they're a character in the story too.

A shadowy figure followed me.

Sometimes the narrator isn't in the story at all. These narrators often know things about the story that the characters don't.

A shadowy figure followed her.

Who the narrator is affects how we see the story.

Rewrite these sentences from Little Red Riding Hood, with Little Red Riding Hood as the narrator. Remember to think about what Red knows about the wolf at different points in the story.

1 Little Red Riding Hood set off. _____

2 She was carrying a basket. _____

3 The wolf crept up and spoke to her. _____

4 Little Red Riding Hood told him where she was going.

_____

5 She stopped to pick some flowers. _____

6 Red went into Grandma's house. _____

7 The wolf was in bed, disguised as Grandma.

_____

8 Red thought her Grandma looked a bit strange.

_____

9 "What big ears you have," said Red. _____

10 Red thought Grandma sounded gruff. _____

11 Red looked more closely. _____

12 The wolf leapt out of the bed and grabbed Red.

_____

13 Red shouted for help. _____

14 A woodcutter burst in. _____

15 He killed the wolf and rescued Grandma.

_____

 *Hurray! Have a Mini T sticker for your certificate.*

Colour in your score.

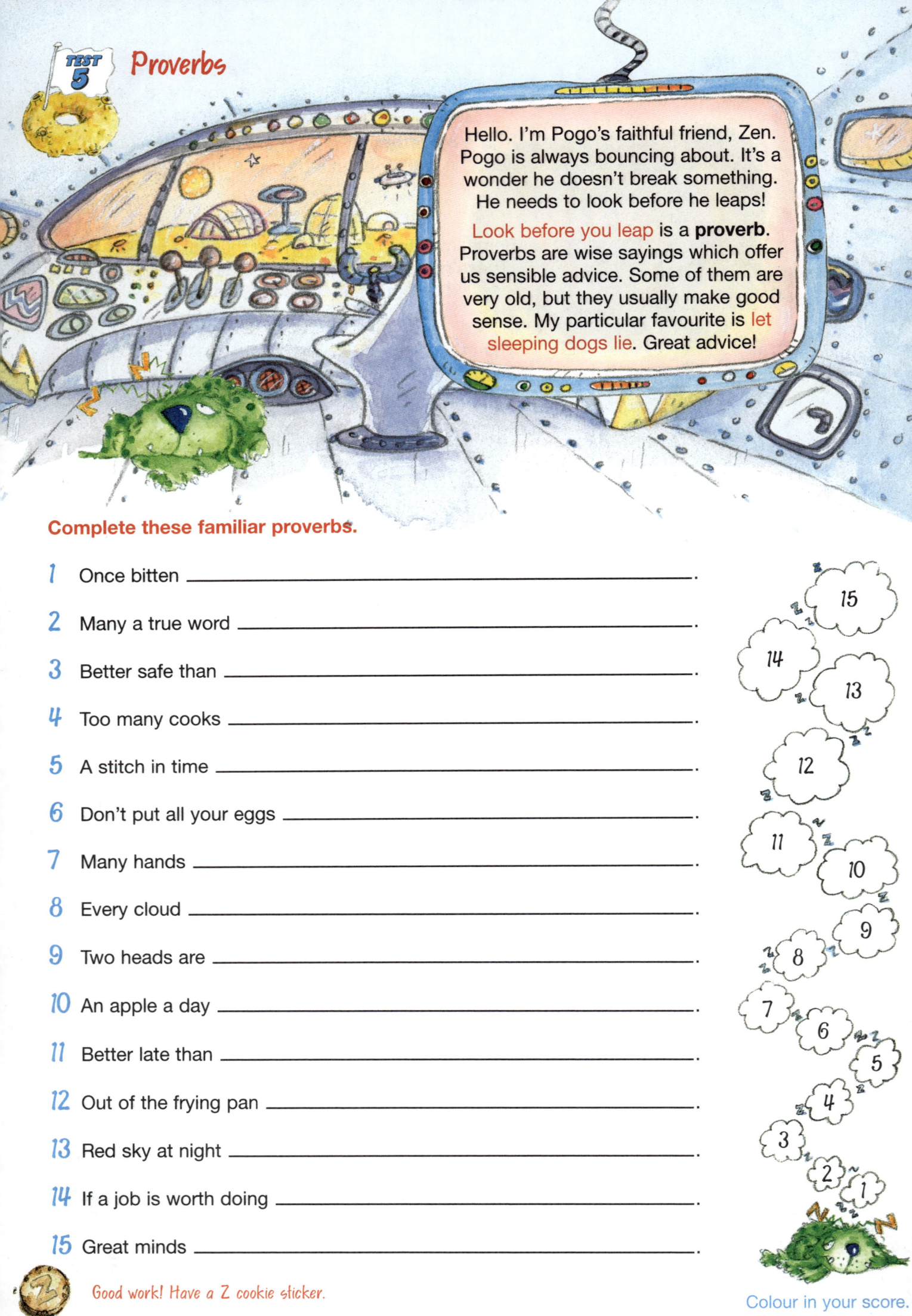

Proverbs

Hello. I'm Pogo's faithful friend, Zen. Pogo is always bouncing about. It's a wonder he doesn't break something. He needs to look before he leaps!

Look before you leap is a **proverb**. Proverbs are wise sayings which offer us sensible advice. Some of them are very old, but they usually make good sense. My particular favourite is let sleeping dogs lie. Great advice!

Complete these familiar proverbs.

1   Once bitten _____.

2   Many a true word _____.

3   Better safe than _____.

4   Too many cooks _____.

5   A stitch in time _____.

6   Don't put all your eggs _____.

7   Many hands _____.

8   Every cloud _____.

9   Two heads are _____.

10 An apple a day _____.

11 Better late than _____.

12 Out of the frying pan _____.

13 Red sky at night _____.

14 If a job is worth doing _____.

15 Great minds _____.

Good work! Have a Z cookie sticker.

Colour in your score.

TEST 6

Argument vocabulary

Everyone here on Dunk is dying to know what visiting Earth is like! I've made lots of notes and now I need to turn them into a powerful **argument** in favour of visiting Earth. Never fear, ZP is here! Connectives like in addition to, however and but will help me to link my various points together, to make the argument easier to understand.

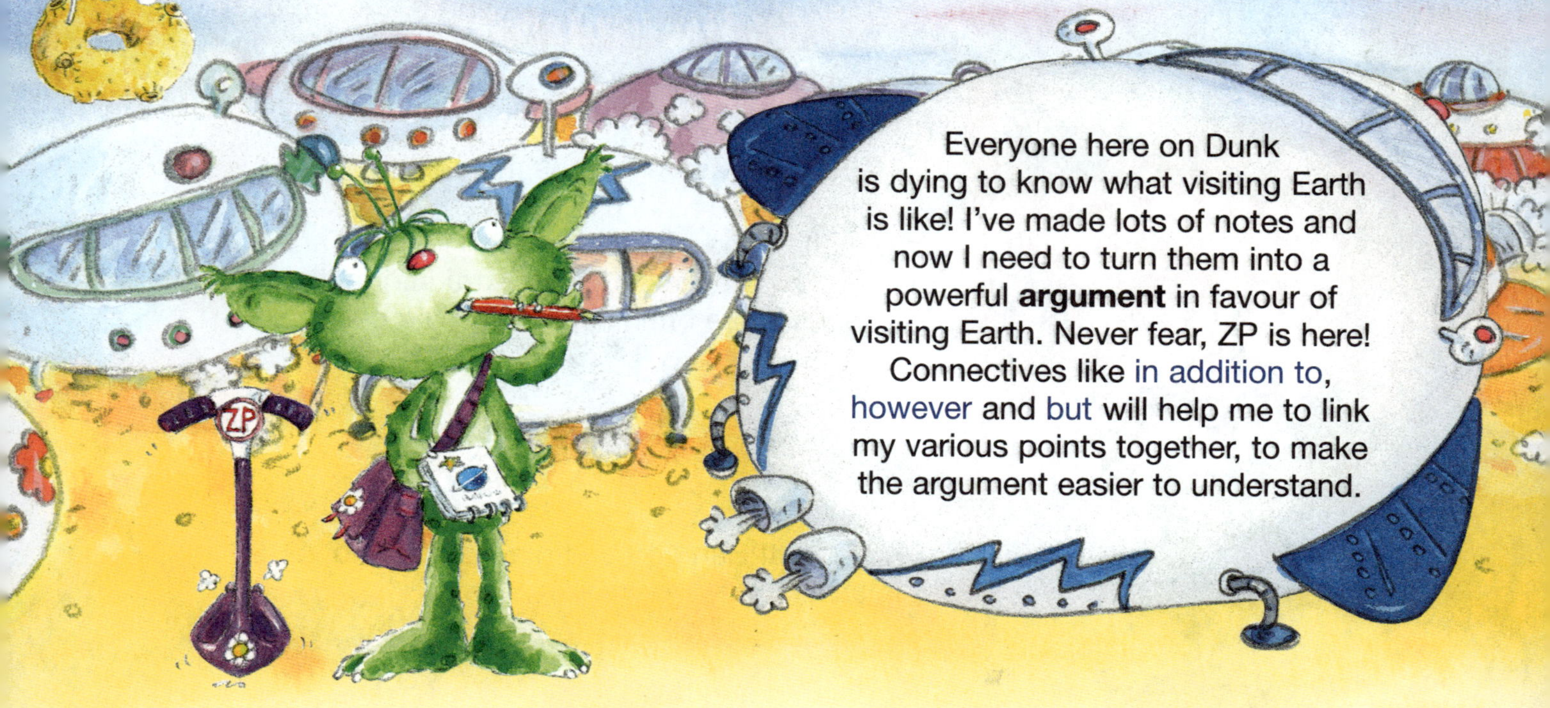

Underline the 15 connective words and phrases in this argument.

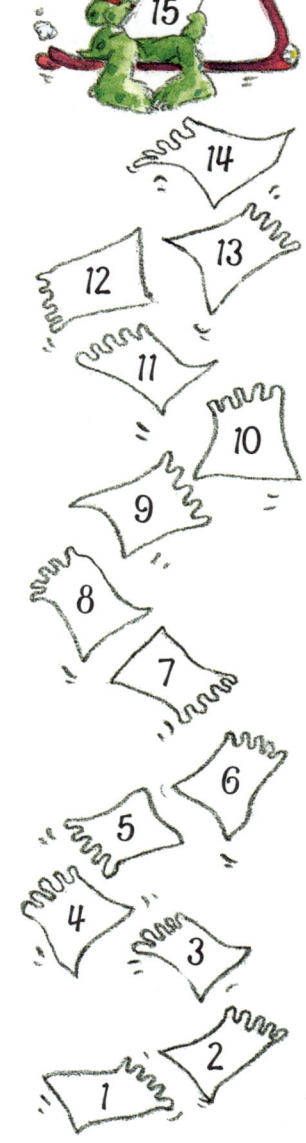

Earth is very far away. However, in a space-mobile, the journey is fairly quick, despite the distance. Whereas on Earth it takes ages to go from place to place, we can get to Earth in minutes. Likewise, we can travel to its neighbouring planets. Nevertheless, Earth is still a favourite destination. What's more, Earth offers a wide range of activities. In addition to its vibrant cities, the planet has beautiful beaches as well as pretty villages. Moreover, Earthlings are known for their friendliness. By comparison, Earth's neighbours are very dull and so are rarely visited.

In contrast to places like Mars and Saturn, a trip to Earth is a real experience. Furthermore, the friendly Earthlings will ensure you have a holiday to remember. As a result, places on the space-mobile are booked up quickly.

Be that as it may, many aliens are still reluctant to visit this lovely planet. But with new shuttle routes operating soon, this is set to change.

15
14
13
12
11
10
9
8
7
6
5
4
3
2
1

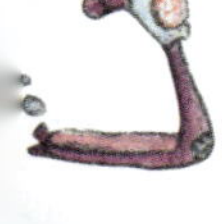

You're zippy! Have a scooter sticker.

Colour in your score.

Complex sentences

Hi, I'm Nok. Err, what? **Complex sentences** really tangle my antennae!

A complex sentence has more than one clause. The main clause gives the key information and makes sense on its own, and the subordinate clause gives extra information. The clauses are often separated by a comma.

(subordinate clause)

Switching on her radio,
Twinx danced around the bedroom.

(main clause)

Oh I get it! Can I go and play football now?

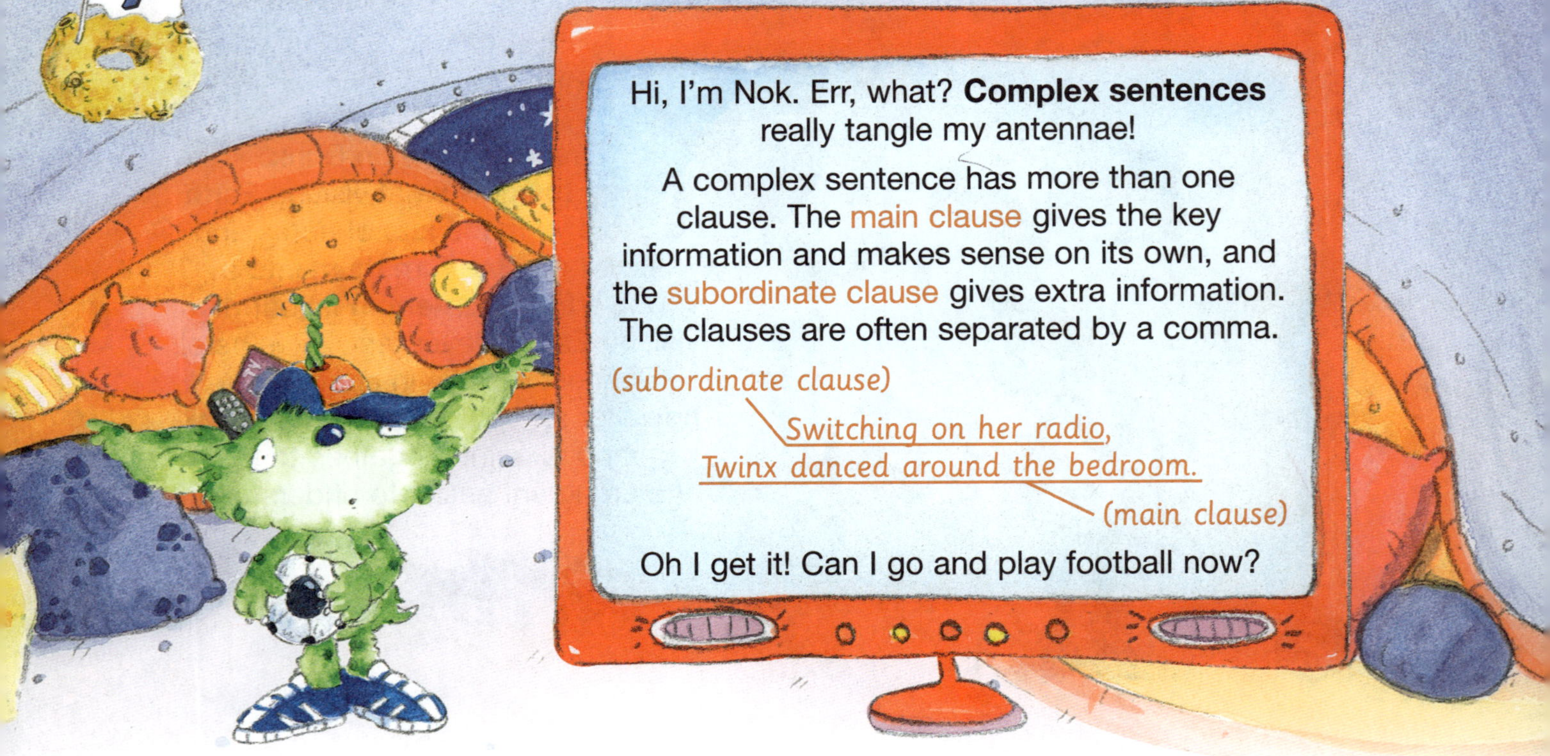

Add a comma to each sentence, to separate the main and subordinate clause, then underline the main clause.

1 Zen fell asleep falling into his cookie bowl.

2 After tidying her bedroom Twinx had room to dance.

3 Pogo loves to bounce even when he is tired.

4 Zing plays his music loud enjoying the noise.

5 Nok grabbed his football before racing out of the door.

6 Zara P checked her jet-scooter preparing for a race.

7 The space-mobile took off heading for Earth.

8 Twinx played with Mini T despite having homework to do.

9 Pogo bounced in leaving dirty spring marks all over the floor.

10 Looking carefully you can see Dunk through a telescope.

11 The aliens won the competition sending in the best entry.

12 Feeling excited Zing pulled on his new trainers.

13 Zara P writes information in her notebook so she can read it later.

14 Nok was man of the match scoring the winning goal.

15 Running home in the rain Twinx got soaked.

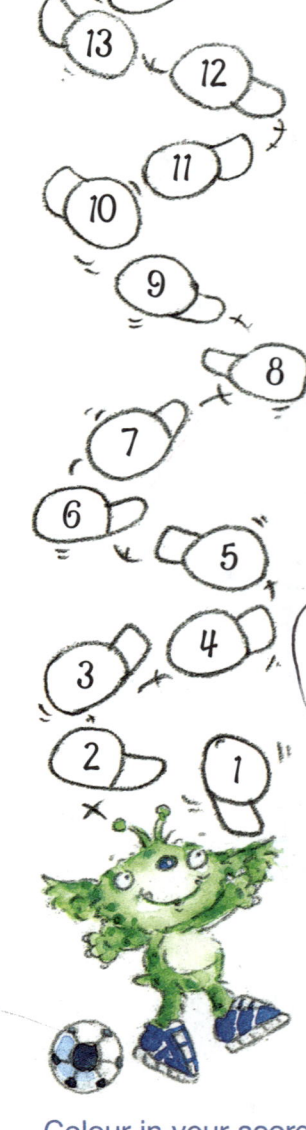

Goal! Have a football sticker.

Colour in your score.

All our rubbish is sorted to make fuel for the space-mobile.

Sorting is useful when you're reading too. It helps you to summarise texts, to make them more manageable, or to make notes of the key points.

> 1. Twinx is practising her ballet because she is getting ready for an exam.
> 2. Twinx is practising for a ballet exam.
> 3. Twinx – practising – ballet exam

You can also edit your own writing, to take out any unnecessary bits. Cool!

Underline the key words or phrases that would help you to summarise or make notes from these sentences.

1 The space-mobile is due to leave Dunk at 8.30am tomorrow.

2 Pogo's trainers have springs on them, which help him to bounce.

3 Zen finds it difficult to stay awake unless he eats lots of Z cookies.

4 Zara P can get about really quickly, because of her jet scooter.

5 The planet the aliens live on is called Dunk and it is in another galaxy.

6 Zing downloads music onto his mp3 player so he can listen to it later.

7 Twinx loves Mini T, because she thinks Mini T looks just like her.

8 Pogo and Nok go to play football in the crater fields every Friday.

9 Zara P's notebook is full of information that she has written down.

10 Zen was snoring so loudly, you could hear it next door!

11 From Dunk, Earth looks just like a big blue and green football.

12 The stars around Dunk shine very brightly, especially at night.

13 Twinx's radio plays music so she can practise her ballet.

14 Nok scored three goals in his football match last Tuesday.

15 Pogo keeps Z cookies for Zen in his backpack.

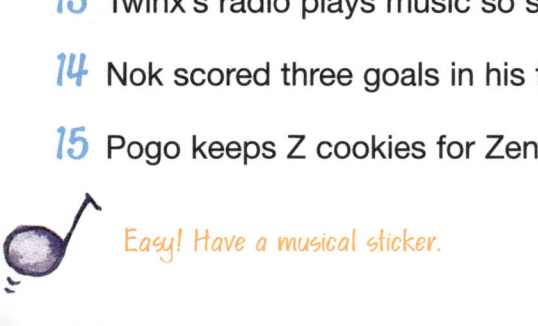

Easy! Have a musical sticker.

Colour in your score.

Writing balanced arguments

Mini T is my best friend and we agree about everything, so writing a **balanced argument** is really tricky for me!

A balanced argument has to include views on both sides, so people can read it and make up their own minds. You use connectives like but and however to join up your points. Hurray!

Here are three arguments in favour of five different topics.
Now think of three arguments against each topic, to balance things up.

For   **Against**

Space travel

1 We can visit new places.   _____

2 We may make scientific discoveries.   _____

3 We might meet other life forms.   _____

Girls playing football with boys

4 Girls can play as well as boys.   _____

5 Everyone needs to keep fit.   _____

6 It will help to produce top
   women footballers.   _____

Having to do homework

7 It helps you learn more quickly.   _____

8 It allows parents to get involved.   _____

9 It frees up time at school for
   fun things.   _____

Having a TV in your bedroom

10 You don't have to watch what
    everyone else is watching.   _____

11 It helps to prevent arguments about
    what to watch.   _____

12 You can watch TV in bed.   _____

Using public transport

13 It is better for the environment.   _____

14 You can travel with all your friends.   _____

15 You don't have to pay to run a car.   _____

Hurray! Have a Mini T sticker.

Colour in your score.

Conditionals

Boing, boing, boing! Words or phrases that show that one thing happening depends on another, are called **conditionals**. They can be connectives, like if or then, or verbs like should or may.

Zen **may** get fat **if** he eats all these Z cookies.

I'd better not let him, then!

Underline the conditional words or phrases in these sentences.

1 If I save up, I can buy a TV.

2 Going to the cinema would be really exciting.

3 We will be late if we do not hurry.

4 It will be too dark to see unless we put the light on.

5 Should Nok win the match, he will be over the moon.

6 If he is hungry, Zen loves eating Z cookies.

7 If he puts his trainers on, Pogo can bounce really high.

8 If Zing plays his music too loudly, people will be cross.

9 Assuming she remembers, Zara P is bringing home cakes for tea.

10 The comet may be visible from Earth soon.

11 Meeting new people can make Twinx feel shy.

12 Providing he gets his Z cookies, Zen will stay awake.

13 In a bouncing competition, Pogo could win first prize.

14 Twinx missed the space-mobile as a result of oversleeping.

15 Zen's team may win the trophy.

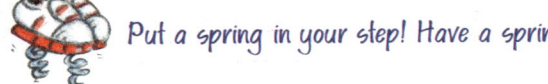

Put a spring in your step! Have a springy sticker.

Colour in your score.

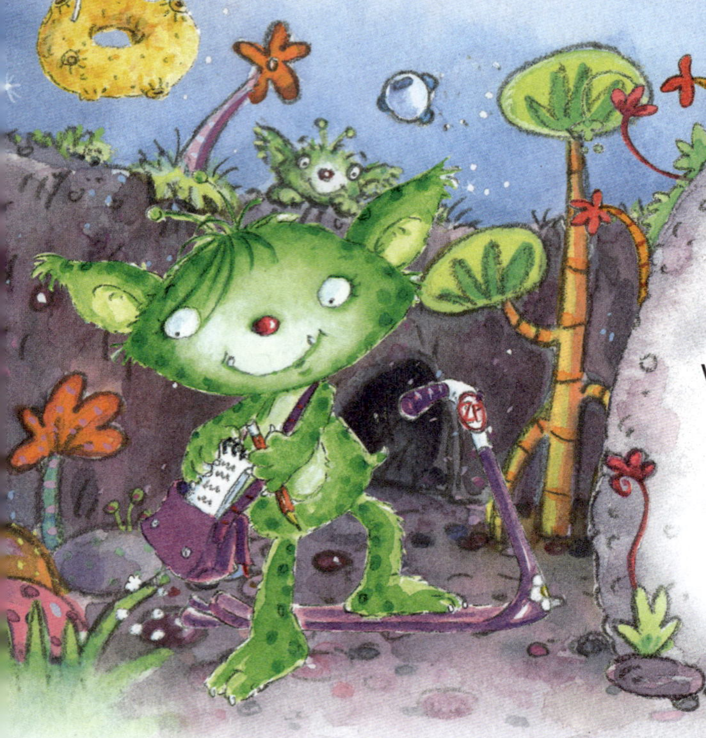

Do you find spelling some words tricky? Never fear, ZP is here! **Mnemonics** are clever ways to remember difficult spellings.

Often they highlight a difficult part of a word that people often spell incorrectly.

*Landfill is hard **on** the envir**on**ment.*

Once you know how they work, you can make up mnemonics for any word you find hard to spell.

Zip, zip, zip!

These mnemonics highlight the part of the word that is easy to spell incorrectly. Draw lines to match up the two halves of the mnemonics.

1 Fri<u>end</u>s

2 <u>Ten</u> doughnuts would be

3 <u>Who</u> ate the

4 They were <u>wed</u>

5 Com<u>b</u> your hair

6 There is a <u>rat</u>

7 The <u>secret</u>ary

8 <u>Cry</u>

9 Hi<u>story</u>

10 Halloween brings <u>hosts</u> of

11 The engine <u>dies</u> when it runs out of

12 Station<u>e</u>ry is things like

13 It's <u>on</u> the tip of my

14 The Fe<u>bru</u>ary weather is

15 <u>Here</u>,

a in sep<u>a</u>r<u>a</u>te.

b <u>cry</u>stal tears.

c is the <u>story</u> of the past.

d <u>who</u>le cake?

e <u>g</u>hosts.

f <u>e</u>nvelopes.

g <u>dies</u>el.

h stick with you until the <u>end</u>.

i t<u>on</u>gue.

j <u>bru</u>tal.

k on a <u>Wed</u>nesday.

l <u>t</u>here and everyw<u>here</u>.

m keeps a <u>secret</u>.

n <u>b</u>efore you go out.

o fatt<u>en</u>ing.

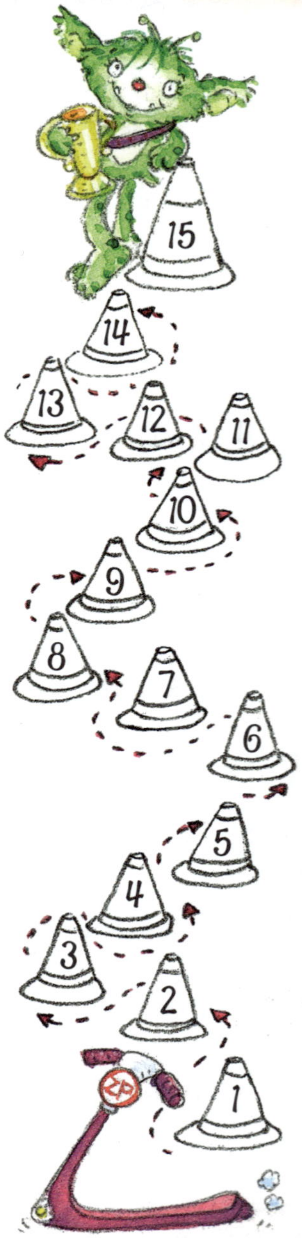

 You're zippy! Have a scooter sticker.

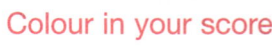

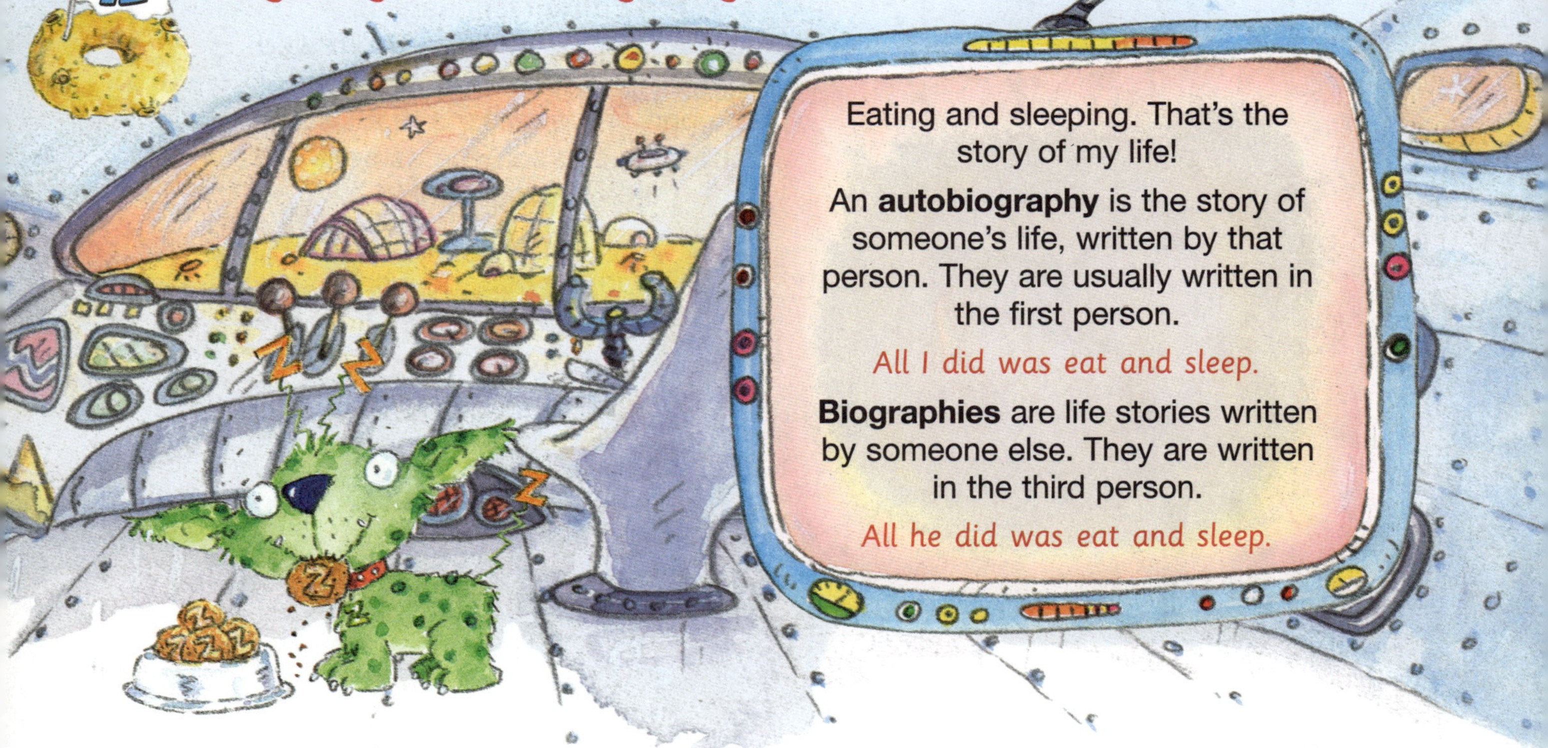

Eating and sleeping. That's the story of my life!

An **autobiography** is the story of someone's life, written by that person. They are usually written in the first person.

All I did was eat and sleep.

Biographies are life stories written by someone else. They are written in the third person.

All he did was eat and sleep.

Write A for autobiography or B for biography by each of the sentences.

1 My space-mobile engine spluttered and died.

2 I watched the eclipse from my window.

3 She lived on a planet called Dunk.

4 We lived in a small town on Dunk.

5 She joined the space federation when she was twenty.

6 He was one of the first alien settlers on Earth.

7 My mother taught at the space academy on Dunk.

8 He designed a telescope capable of seeing craters on Mars.

9 My first job was working on the booster rockets for the shuttle.

10 My father spent months at a time on the space station.

11 She governed Dunk firmly, but fairly.

12 I became fascinated by the variety of life I saw on Earth.

13 Her contribution to astronomy led a star to be named after her.

14 I remember wondering, as a child, what Earth was like.

15 He predicted the appearance of the comet, using complex maths.

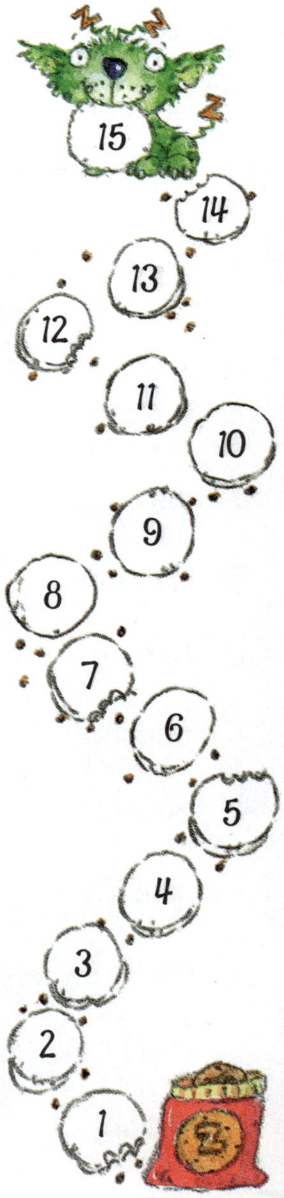

15 14 13 12 11 10 9 8 7 6 5 4 3 2 1

Good work! Have a Z cookie sticker.

Colour in your score.

TEST 13

Word origins

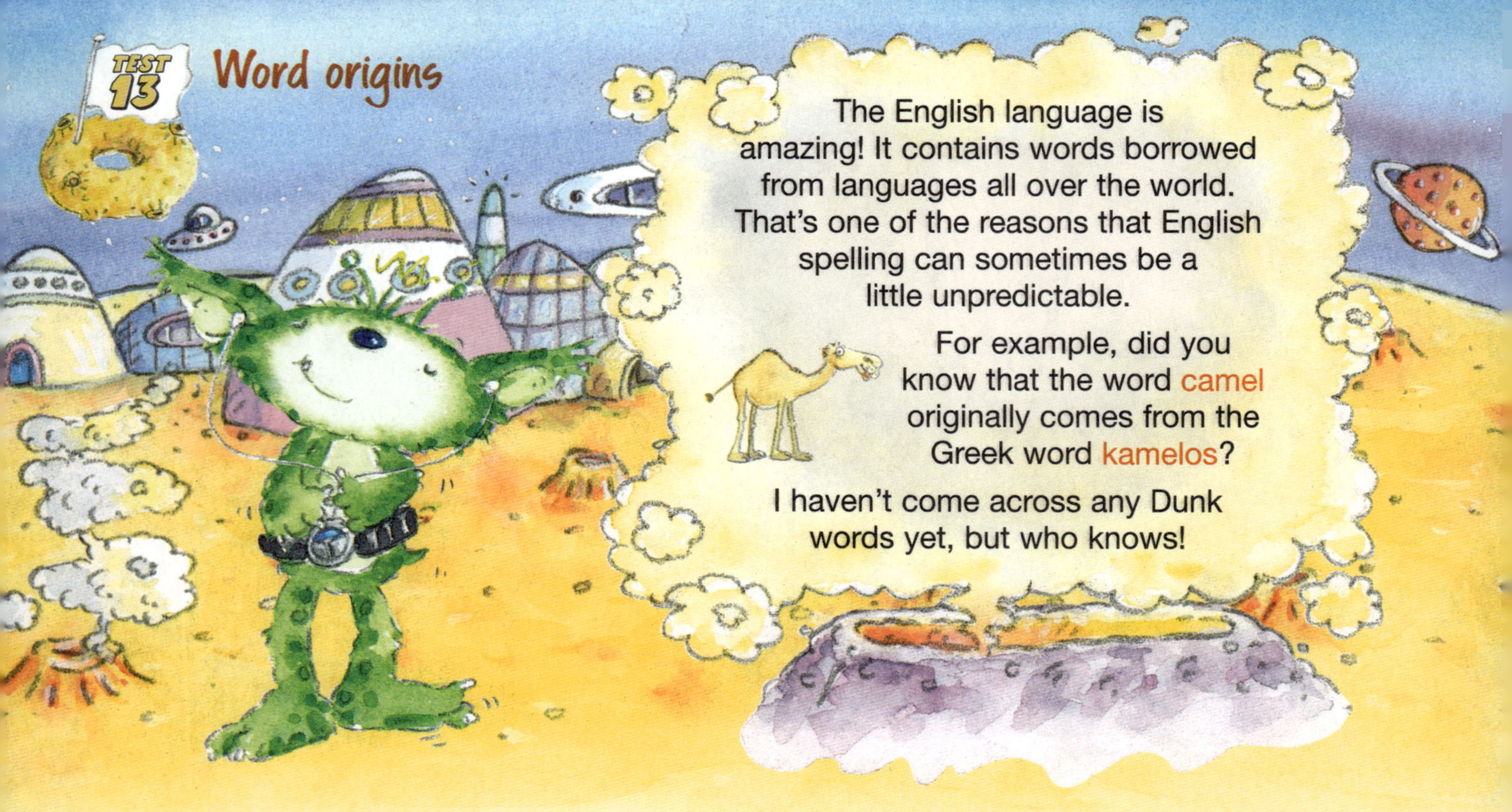

The English language is amazing! It contains words borrowed from languages all over the world. That's one of the reasons that English spelling can sometimes be a little unpredictable.

For example, did you know that the word camel originally comes from the Greek word kamelos?

I haven't come across any Dunk words yet, but who knows!

Follow the lines to find the origin of each of these words.

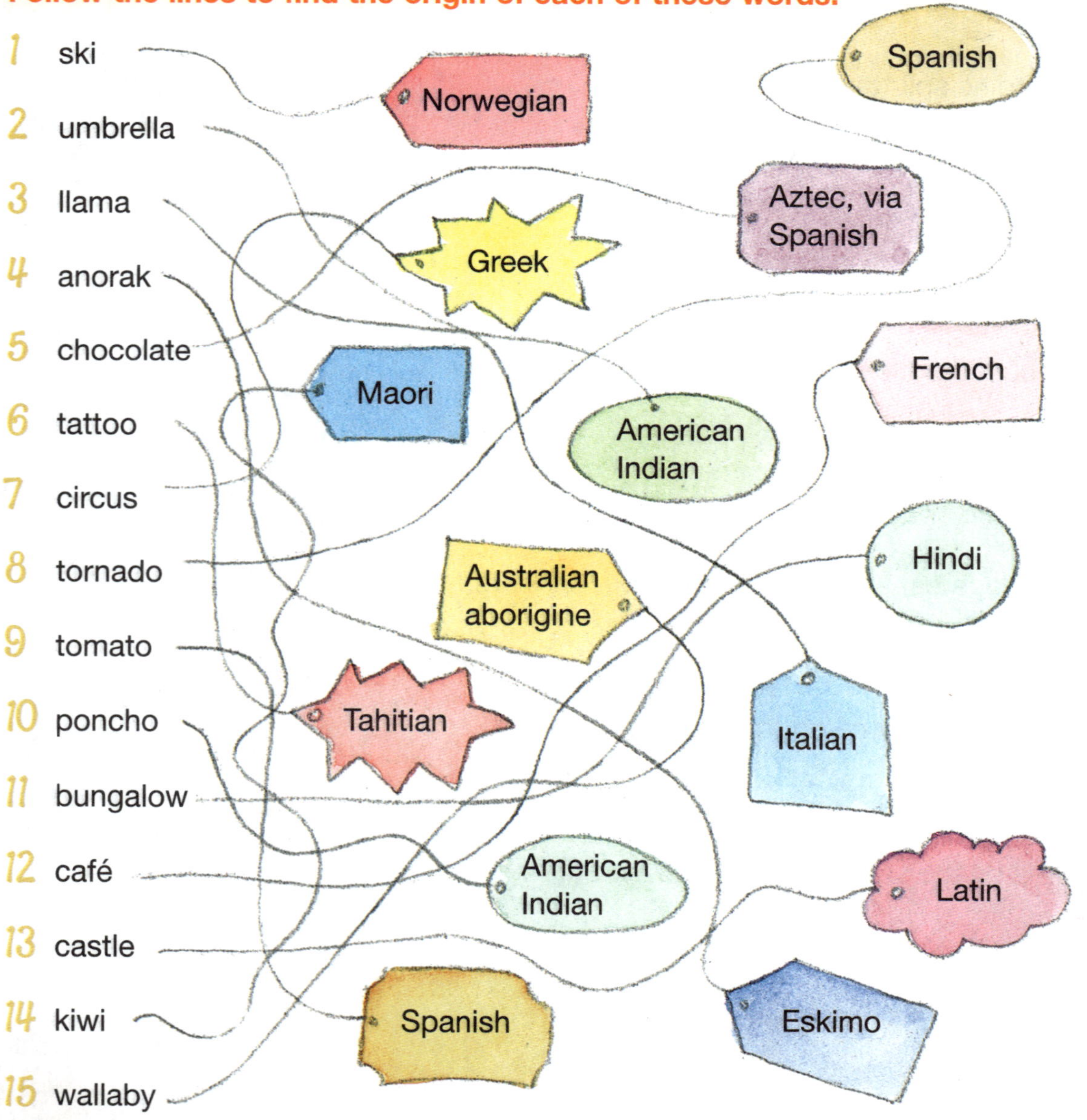

1 ski
2 umbrella
3 llama
4 anorak
5 chocolate
6 tattoo
7 circus
8 tornado
9 tomato
10 poncho
11 bungalow
12 café
13 castle
14 kiwi
15 wallaby
Spanish
Norwegian
Aztec, via Spanish
Greek
French
Maori
American Indian
Hindi
Australian aborigine
Italian
Tahitian
American Indian
Latin
Spanish
Eskimo

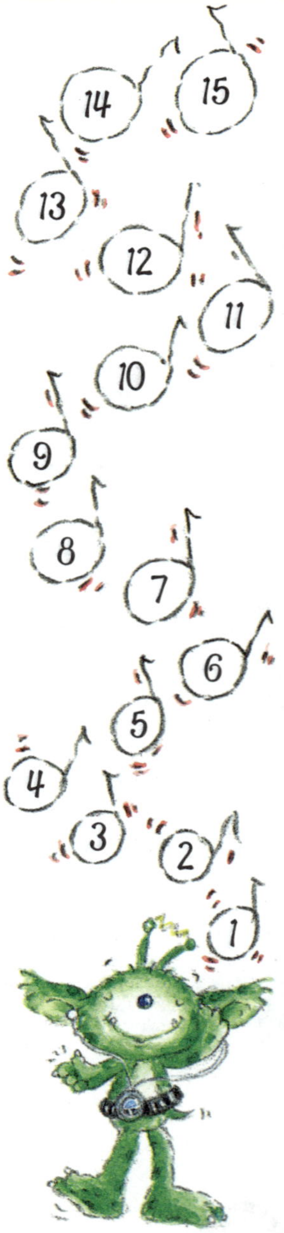

1
2
3
4
5
6
7
8
9
10
11
12
13
14
15

Easy! Have a musical sticker.

Colour in your score.

I have a recipe in my notebook that I want to adapt for Twinx. When you **adapt text**, you have to think about who is going to read it. Twinx is the youngest, so I need to keep it simple, and only use words she can read and understand. So I might say 'mix the ingredients', instead of 'combine the ingredients'. I also need to think about what she can do safely, for example, reminding her to get help with the oven. I'll just make a note of that…

Adapt these instructions so they are suitable for a younger reader.

1 Locate all of the ingredients. _____

2 Select a sizeable mixing bowl. _____

3 Pre-heat the oven to 180°C. _____
_____

4 With a sharp grater, remove the zest from a lemon. _____
_____

5 Use a sharp knife to slice the lemon in half. _____
_____

6 Extract the juice from the lemon by squeezing it. _____
_____

7 Discard the lemon skin. _____

8 Blend the lemon zest and juice with the sugar and butter. _____
_____

9 Gradually introduce 3 eggs. _____

10 Stir continuously and vigorously. _____

11 Employing great care, gently stir in the flour. _____
_____

12 Transfer the mixture to a cake tin. _____

13 Place the tin inside the oven. _____

14 The cooking time is estimated to be 25 minutes. _____
_____

15 Permit the cake to cool thoroughly before removing it from the cake tin.
_____

You're zippy! Have a scooter sticker.

Colour in your score.

Checking your spelling

Spelling really tangles my antennae! Lucky there are lots of ways to check I've got it right. Dictionaries can help, and so can computers. When I spell a word wrong on my computer, it is underlined in red. The computer even suggests how it should be spelt. It won't spot the wrong homophone, though, like weight instead of wait. If it suggests several different words, you just have to take care to pick the right one!

Circle a word from the suggestions to replace the incorrectly spelt words, which are underlined in red.

1   I did not mean to brak the window.   bark   brake   break

2   Twinx loves the ballet Swon Lake.   Swoon   Sown   Swan

3   Pogo threw a Z cookie for Zen to cath.   catch   cat   cash

4   The aliens love to visit plaet Earth.   plait   plate   planet

5   Nok watched the rocke take off.   rocker   rocket   rocked

6   Dunk and Earth are very dfferent.   different   deferent   efferent

7   Zara P had a grat time on Earth.   grit   grate   great

8   All Zen cares abot is eating and sleeping.   abbot   abut   about

9   The aliens boarded the space-obile.   mobile   bile   oblige

10 Nok's team wun the football match.   won   win   wan

11 Twinx listened to her rado.   radon   redo   radio

12 The spae rocket headed for Earth.   space   spade   spare

13 Zen is bord if he cannot play football.   board   bard   bored

14 Twinx got ost among the craters.   oust   oat   lost

15 Zara P is very brany.   briny   brandy   brainy

Goal! Have a football sticker.

Colour in your score.

This turn is my favourite dance move! You can use it in so many different dances. **Root words** like turn are really useful for spelling too. Once you have learnt to spell them once, you can use them to help you spell lots of other words too.

re**turn**   **turn**table   **turn**ing

Hurray! Come on, Mini T, let's dance!

Write the root words on the ribbons.

1	delight	lightning	slight
2	folding	folder	unfold
3	viewpoint	preview	review
4	remove	movement	moveable
5	despite	spiteful	respite
6	freshly	refresh	freshest
7	harmful	unharmed	harmless
8	replay	playful	display
9	unclear	clearly	cleared
10	marked	remark	marking
11	handful	underhand	handy
12	restful	unrest	rested
13	building	rebuild	builder
14	television	revision	visionary
15	loveable	beloved	glove

Hurray! Have a Mini T sticker.

Colour in your score.

That star is keeping me awake. It's shining **its** bright light right into my eyes!

Did you notice that one **it's** above had an apostrophe in it and one **its** didn't. Relax! It's easy to know which one to use. You use **it's** with an apostrophe when you mean 'it is'. The apostrophe shows some letters have been taken away. You use **its** without an apostrophe when you mean something belonging to it. See? You could do this in your… zzz.

Write its or it's to complete these sentences.

1 _____ very cold on Dunk tonight.

2 Earth is great, but _____ very far from Dunk.

3 Twinx's radio stopped working, because _____ batteries ran down.

4 Pogo should stop bouncing, but _____ too much fun!

5 The huge space-mobile cast _____ shadow across Dunk.

6 Twinx practises her ballet a lot, because _____ hard to get right.

7 The Earth spins on _____ axis.

8 The space rocket left _____ vapour trail across the sky.

9 The aliens think _____ fun to play in the craters.

10 Zing's music player works fine, but _____ earphones are broken.

11 _____ not possible to see Dunk from Earth without a telescope.

12 Nok thinks _____ great to score a goal.

13 The space-mobile closed _____ doors just before the aliens arrived.

14 The aliens won the competition, because they were _____ best entrants.

15 _____ fun to ride on a jet scooter.

 *Good work! Have a Z cookie sticker.*

Colour in your score.

Brackets

> Boing, boing, boing! My trainers (which have springs on them) help me to bounce really high!
>
> Like my trainers, brackets can be really useful. You can use them to bounce extra information into a sentence, but if you take them away, the sentence still makes sense. Look –
>
> Bouncing about **(unless you're careful)** can be dangerous!
>
> Bouncing about can be dangerous.

Cross out the incorrectly placed brackets (and the words inside them).

1   The space-mobile (full of aliens) headed for (full of aliens) Earth.

2   Pogo's (with springs on) trainers (with springs on) were under his bed.

3   Earth (seen through a telescope) looks green (seen through a telescope) and blue.

4   The meteor shower (and astral winds) continued (and astral winds) all day.

5   Z cookies (fed to him regularly) keep (fed to him regularly) Zen awake.

6   Twinx's hair ribbons (all tangled up) were in a pile on (all tangled up) the floor.

7   Zara P put (full of information) her notebook (full of information) in her bag.

8   Nok's football boots (and soaking wet) were filthy (and soaking wet).

9   After lunch (without his springy trainers) Nok and Pogo (without his springy trainers) played football.

10   Twinx's radio (which she takes everywhere with her) played music (which she takes everywhere with her).

11   Zing sat (looking cool) by the (looking cool) crater.

12   Zen fell (as usual) asleep (as usual) after tea.

13   Zing's music player (which he bought on Earth) is the (which he bought on Earth) latest model.

14   Zara P's jet-scooter (at top speed) gets (at top speed) her home in no time.

15   Pogo's (stuffed with Z cookies) rucksack (stuffed with Z cookies) was heavy.

Put a spring in your step! Have a springy sticker.

Colour in your score.

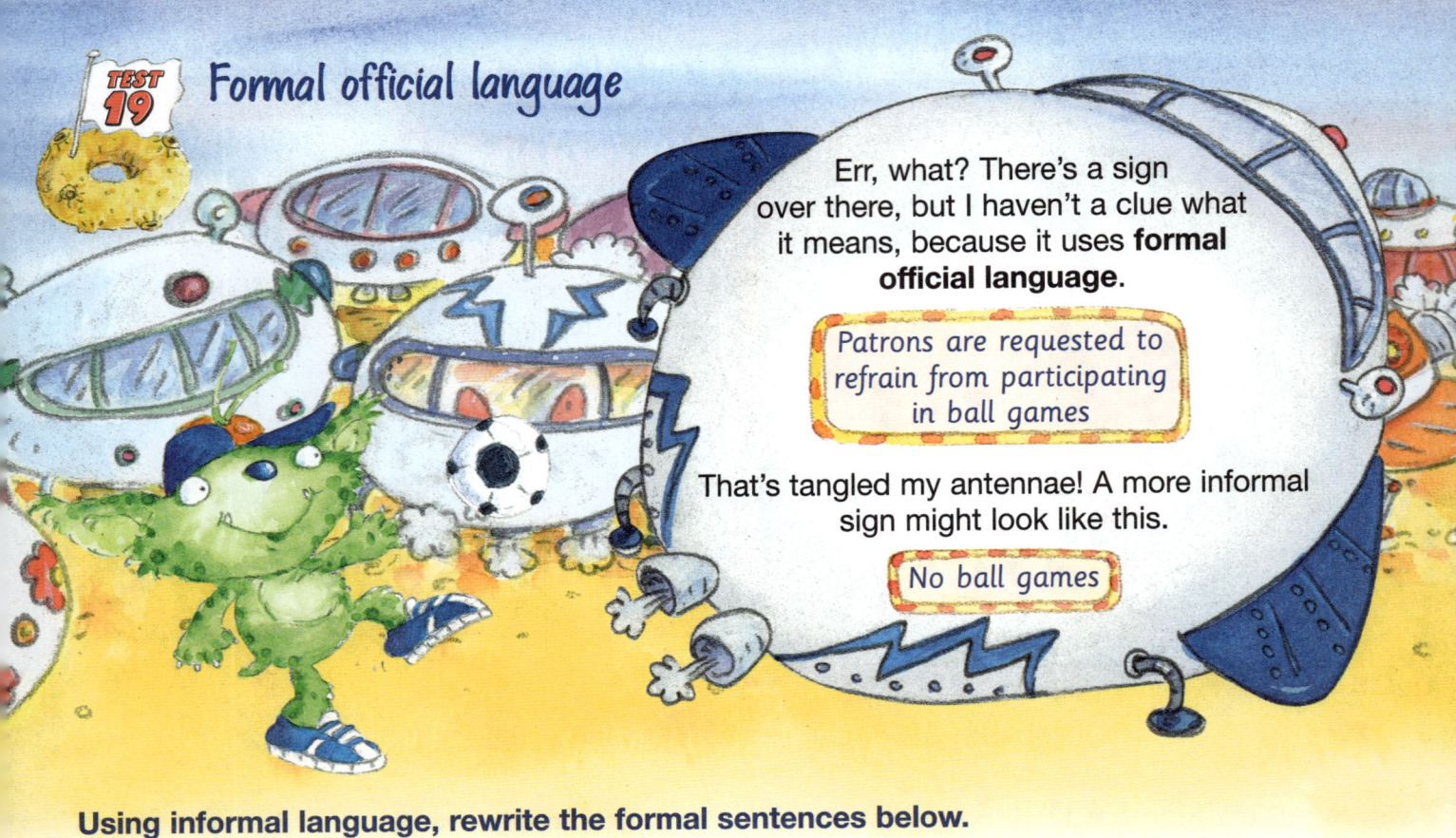

Err, what? There's a sign over there, but I haven't a clue what it means, because it uses **formal official language**.

Patrons are requested to refrain from participating in ball games

That's tangled my antennae! A more informal sign might look like this.

No ball games

Using informal language, rewrite the formal sentences below.

1 Parking is prohibited. _____

2 Dogs are not permitted. _____

3 Not for human consumption. _____

4 In the event of a fire… _____

5 … please vacate the premises. _____

6 Management are not liable… _____

7 … for lost or damaged property. _____

8 Please retain your ticket… _____

9 … to gain a refund. _____

10 Public conveniences… _____

11 … are located around the premises. _____

12 Orders will be despatched… _____

13 … on receipt of payment. _____

14 Mislaid parking tickets… _____

15 … will incur a release fee. _____

Goal! Have a football sticker.

Colour in your score.

Making new words

Prefixes and suffixes are zippy little things. Each one has its own meaning, so by adding them to words, or joining them together, you can make up zippy new words. Never fear, ZP is here! I've made a note of the meaning of some common prefixes.

hydro & aqua = water   crypto = hidden

macro = large   sub = below

pyro = fire   micro = small

poly = many   chrom = colour

Draw lines to match up the definitions with the made-up words.

1   a type of pond-dwelling cattle

2   an enormous honey-making insect

3   a tree whose leaves are flames

4   an ocean-dwelling pig

5   a device to allow sound to travel through water

6   an elephant with five trunks

7   a hidden entrance

8   a city built below the Earth's surface

9   footwear for Earthlings with tiny feet

10   something covered in many dots

11   a box designed to contain a fire

12   a hidden code

13   a snail which lives below the surface

14   a device designed to protect you from water

15   a detergent bar which changes colour as it's used

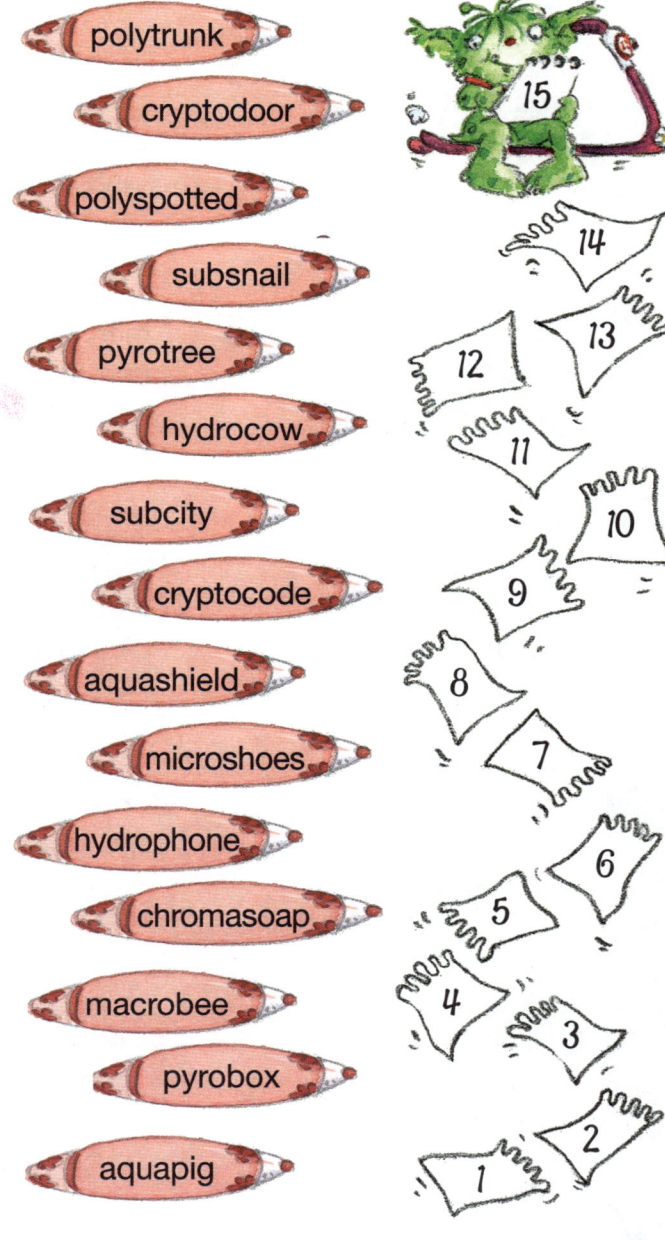

polytrunk

cryptodoor

polyspotted

subsnail

pyrotree

hydrocow

subcity

cryptocode

aquashield

microshoes

hydrophone

chromasoap

macrobee

pyrobox

aquapig

You're zippy! Have a scooter sticker.

Colour in your score.

Unstressed vowels

Wow! No matter how hard I listen to some words, I can't hear all of the letters in them. Lots of longer words contain vowels that we just don't pronounce at all!

jewellery ✔   jewellry ✗

With other words, it can be hard to hear which vowel sound the word contains.

carpet ✔   carpit ✗

Words like these can be hard to spell, so I have to learn them carefully.

Circle the correctly spelt word on each of the CDs.

1
parlament
parliament
parlement

2
conference
confrence
confarence

3
tempreture
temparature
temperature

4
frightening
frightning
frightaning

5
memrable
memorable
memerable

6
genrally
genarally
generally

7
deafning
deafaning
deafening

8
desperate
desprate
desparate

9
seprate
separate
seperate

10
easly
easaly
easily

11
holiday
holaday
holleday

12
libry
librery
library

13
literature
litrature
litarature

14
offring
offering
offaring

15
intrested
intarested
interested

Easy! Have a musical sticker.

Colour in your score.

Personification

I'm telling Mini T a story. It contains lots of **personification**. That's when the writer describes something as if it were a person.

The Moon **gazed down** on the princess.

The Moon can't really gaze, because it's a lump of rock, but describing it that way helps me to imagine what it looks like. Hurray!

Underline the 15 uses of personification in this story.

The knight's armour winked in the moonlight as he approached the castle. The drawbridge was lowered like a huge wooden tongue in the castle's great stone mouth. Its empty windows stared down at the knight from sleeping turrets. Ancient walls viewed the trespasser with hostility, while roosting birds muttered their disapproval.

The wind whispered around the crumbling walls, as the knight approached a crooked doorway crouched in a corner of the courtyard. It was framed by lanterns in which pale yellow flames danced.

Beyond the doorway, an old staircase stumbled its way crookedly upwards into the waiting darkness. Climbing, the knight's feet disturbed loose stones which chased each other back down the stairs, chattering as they went.

The castle had kept its secret for 100 years. Was it about to confide in this stranger?

Oh well done! Have a Mini T sticker.

Colour in your score.

Adjectives

Z cookies are so tasty! Tasty, tastier and tastiest are all **adjectives**. Adjectives are words we use to describe nouns.

Comparative adjectives, like tastier, allow us to compare two things; this Z cookie is tastier than that one.

Superlative adjectives describe the most of a particular quality that something can be; this is the tastiest Z cookie of all!

See? You could do this in your… zzz.

Fill in the missing adjectives in the chart.

	Adjective	Comparative adjective	Superlative adjective
1	small	smaller	
2		older	oldest
3	big		biggest
4	silly	sillier	
5		warmer	warmest
6	safe	safer	
7	hungry		hungriest
8		stranger	strangest
9	bright		brightest
10	dark	darker	
11	lazy		laziest
12		funnier	funniest
13	sad		saddest
14	late	later	
15		taller	tallest

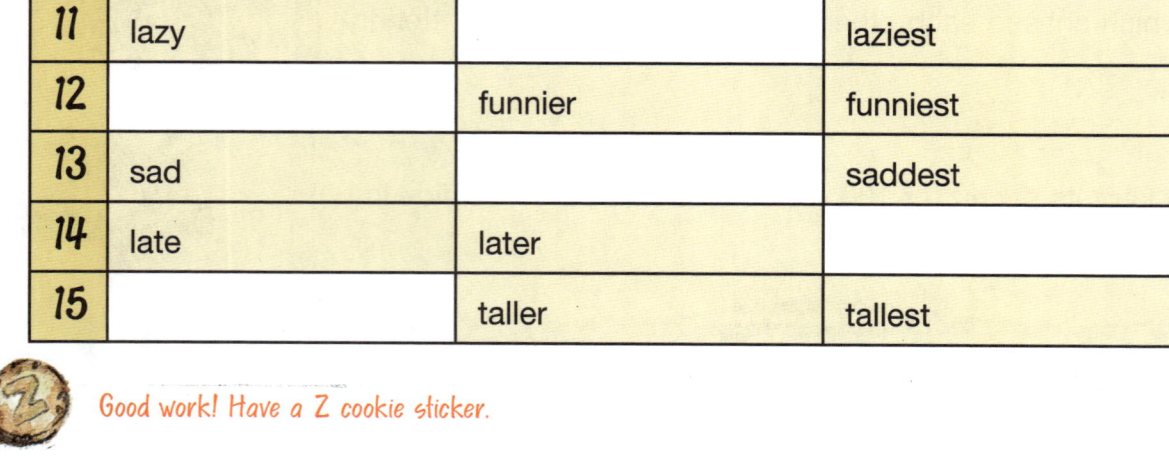

Good work! Have a Z cookie sticker.

Colour in your score.

21/01/14

Boing, boing, boing! Have you ever noticed that stories often bounce between direct speech and reported speech? **Direct speech** is where you quote a person's actual words, using speech punctuation. You can use it to let two characters talk to each other. **Reported speech** allows you to write what someone has said, but without using their actual words, so there are no speech marks.

Rewrite these bits of reported speech as direct speech.

1   Zing said his music was too quiet. _____

2   Zen asked if he could have a Z cookie.

_____

3   Twinx asked where Mini T was. _____

4   Zara P said she was going out. _____

5   Pogo said he liked bouncing. _____

6   Nok said he was off to play football. _____

7   Zing asked if Zara P had seen Zen. _____

8   Twinx asked Zing to fix her radio. _____

9   Zara P asked Pogo to look in her notebook.

_____

10 Nok said that he was confused. _____

11 The alien shopkeeper announced that the shop was closing.

_____

12 Zen grumbled that he was tired. _____

13 Pogo suggested that the aliens should go for a walk.

_____

14 The space-mobile captain said there were no spare seats.

_____

15 Zing asked if Nok liked his new trainers. _____

Put a spring in your step! Have a springy sticker.

Colour in your score.

TEST 25 Fact, fiction and opinion

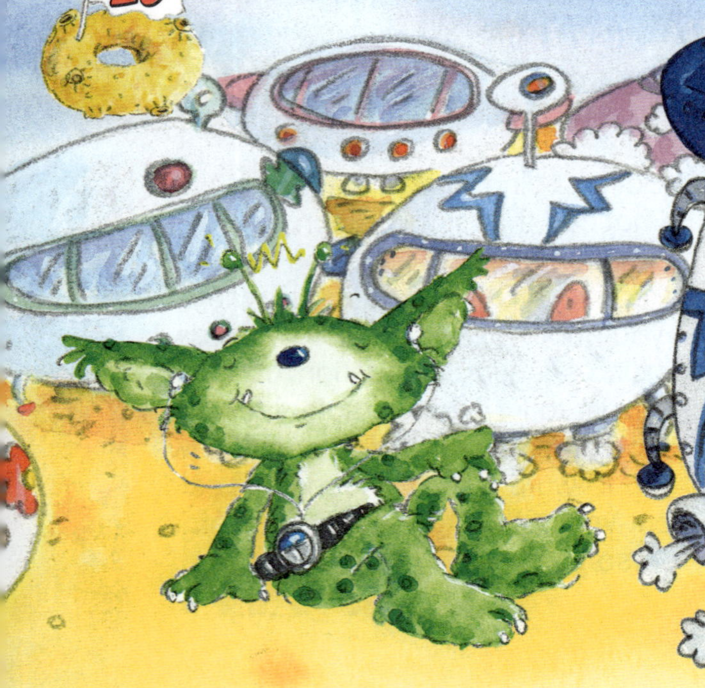

Did you know…
If information you read or hear is true, it's called **fact**.

The Moon is far away.

If information is made up, like a story, it's called **fiction**.

The Moon is made of cheese.

If what you read or hear is based on what someone thinks or feels, it's called an **opinion**.

I think the Moon is beautiful.

Get it? Cool!

Write fact, fiction or opinion under each sentence.

1 Humans live on Earth.

2 The world is round.

3 I think Brussels sprouts are delicious.

4 The wise pig built a brick house.

5 Dinosaurs still live on Earth.

6 Nok thinks going to the cinema is fun.

7 Ice is cold.

8 Trees are usually green.

9 Twinx thinks roses smell lovely.

10 I think this book is brilliant.

11 Bears live in houses and eat porridge.

12 Diamonds are precious stones.

13 Beanstalks grow up into the clouds.

14 Pogo thinks pizzas are delicious.

15 A woodcutter rescued a grandmother from the stomach of a wolf.

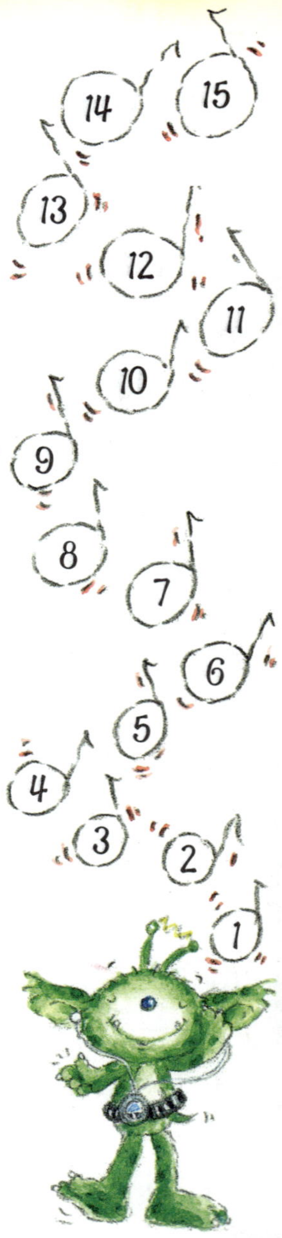

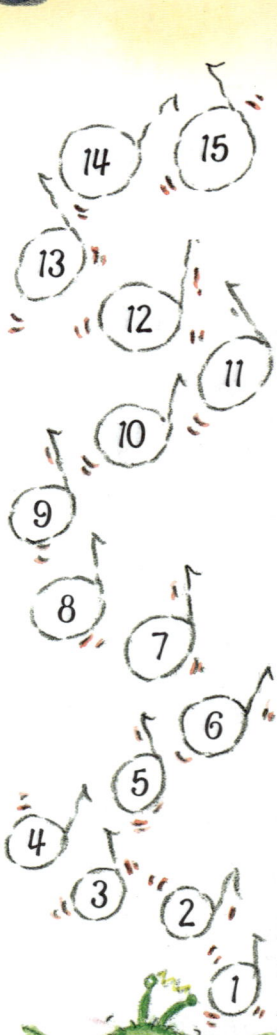

Easy! Have a musical sticker.

Colour in your score.

Luttow → photocopy

Zip, zip, zip! I'm as quick as a flash on my jet-scooter! It lets me fly like a bird! Those are similes, you know. **Similes** compare one thing to another using the words as or like. They are great for creating a picture in your reader's mind. There are lots of familiar similes, or you can make up your own.

Complete these similes. If you don't know the answer, make up one of your own!

1 as busy as a _____

2 as bold as _____

3 sleeping like a _____

4 run like the _____

5 as gentle as a _____

6 swims like a _____

7 as light as a _____

8 pure like the driven _____

9 as white as a _____

10 a face like _____

11 as pretty as a _____

12 smoking like a _____

13 as quiet as a _____

14 eating like a _____

15 climbing like a _____

You're zippy! Have a scooter sticker.

Colour in your score.

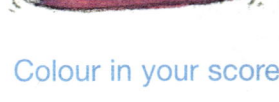

Genre

If you think my music collection is cool, you should see my bookshelves! I have hundreds of books from loads of different genres.

A **genre** is a particular type of writing. Thrillers, science fiction, romance and westerns are all different genres. The genre that a book belongs to will affect the characters, plot, and even the kind of language used. Wow!

Draw a line to join each book to the genre it belongs to.

1 Space Pirates
2 Robin Hood
3 Wagons West
4 Polonius of Pompeii
5 Robot Revenge
6 Apaches Approach
7 The Amazing Shrinking Man
8 On the Trail of Little Big Feather
9 The Sheriff of Cold Creek
10 Into the Future
11 Tales from a Tudor Court
12 Stories of the Blitz
13 Massive Bugs in 2050
14 Tales of a Chimney Sweep
15 Cattle Rustlers at the OK Corral

Science Fiction

Westerns

Historical Fiction

15
14
13
12
11
10
9
8
7
6
5
4
3
2
1

Easy! Have a musical sticker.

Colour in your score.

Visual clues for spelling

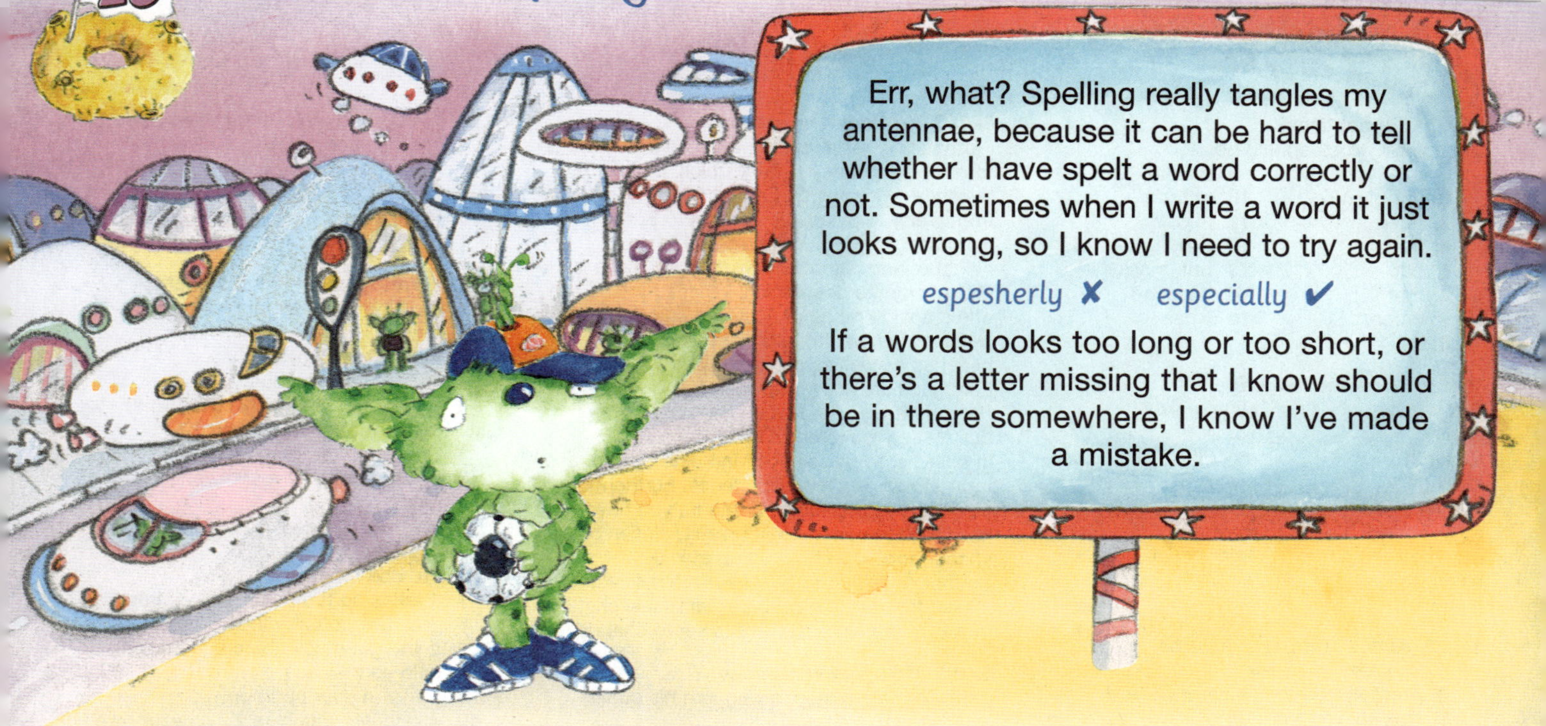

Err, what? Spelling really tangles my antennae, because it can be hard to tell whether I have spelt a word correctly or not. Sometimes when I write a word it just looks wrong, so I know I need to try again.

espesherly ✗   especially ✔

If a words looks too long or too short, or there's a letter missing that I know should be in there somewhere, I know I've made a mistake.

Circle the correctly spelt word, using visual spelling clues to help you.

1. successful
   sucesssful
   sucsfull

2. nesessary
   necessary
   necsessry

3. optimistic
   opimistic
   optimtic

4. transparparent
   transparent
   transprant

5. bounary
   bondary
   boundary

6. micscopic
   microscopic
   microscopopic

7. transpot
   trasport
   transport

8. unbelievable
   unblievable
   unbelievievable

9. realistic
   relistic
   realistik

10. entance
    etrance
    entrance

11. fountin
    fontain
    fountain

12. hospital
    hospial
    hospitial

13. magishan
    magician
    magition

14. magazeen
    maggazine
    magazine

15. troppical
    tropical
    tropickle

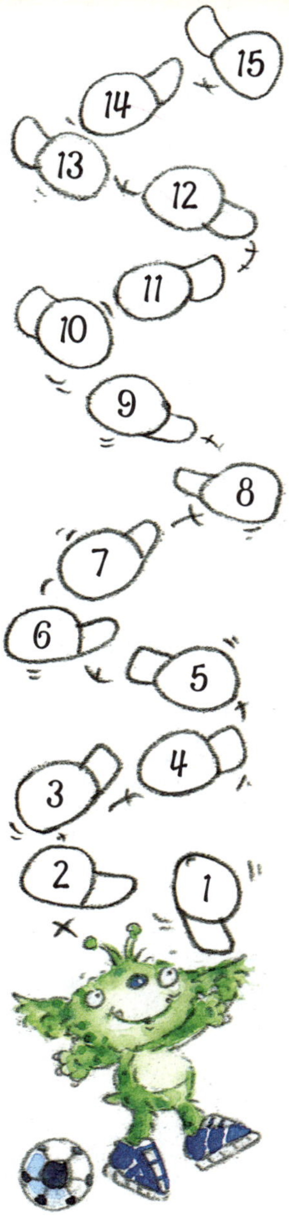

Congratulations! Have a last football sticker for your certificate. He shoots, he scores!

Colour in your score.

Answers

Test 1 Connectives
Underlined words should be:

1	so	9	despite
2	but even so	10	until
3	after	11	and
4	then	12	then
5	but	13	but
6	that	14	because
7	before	15	when
8	as		

Test 2 Changing language

Old words	New words
alas	email
forsooth	smoothie
shilling	podcast
yonder	snowboard
serf	texting
galoshes	solar panel
hither	website
squire	

Test 3 Active and passive verbs
1 Zen ate the cookies.
2 An alien flew the space-mobile.
3 Nok scored a goal.
4 Twinx performed a dance.
5 Zing turned up the music.
6 Zara P owns the notebook.
7 Pogo broke the vase.
8 Twinx held Mini T.
9 The aliens won the competition.
10 Zara P fixed the scooter.
11 Zen made a noise.
12 Pogo dropped the rucksack.
13 The aliens boarded the space-mobile.
14 Pogo played in the crater.
15 Zing put on the trainers.

Test 4 Narrator
1 I set off.
2 I was carrying a basket.
3 The wolf crept up and spoke to me.
4 I told him where I was going.
5 I stopped to pick some flowers.
6 I went into Grandma's house.
7 Grandma was in bed.
8 I thought Grandma looked a bit strange.
9 "What big ears you have," I said.
10 I thought Grandma sounded gruff.
11 I looked more closely.
12 The wolf leapt out of the bed and grabbed me.
13 I shouted for help.
14 A woodcutter burst in.
15 He killed the wolf and rescued Grandma.

Test 5 Proverbs
1 Once bitten **twice shy**.
2 Many a true word **is said in jest**.
3 Better safe than **sorry**.
4 Too many cooks **spoil the broth**.
5 A stitch in time **saves nine**.
6 Don't put all your eggs **in one basket**.
7 Many hands **make light work**.
8 Every cloud **has a silver lining**.
9 Two heads are **better than one**.
10 An apple a day **keeps the doctor away**.
11 Better late than **never**.
12 Out of the frying pan **into the fire**.
13 Red sky at night **shepherds' delight**.
14 If a job is worth doing **it is worth doing well**.
15 Great minds **think alike**.

Test 6 Argument vocabulary
Earth is very far away. However, in a space-mobile, the journey is fairly quick, despite the distance. Whereas on Earth it takes ages to go from place to place, we can get to Earth in minutes. Likewise, we can travel to its neighbouring planets. Nevertheless, Earth is still a favourite destination. What's more, Earth offers a wide range of activities. In addition to its vibrant cities, the planet has beautiful beaches as well as pretty villages. Moreover, Earthlings are known for their friendliness. By comparison, Earth's neighbours are very dull and so are rarely visited.

In contrast to places like Mars and Saturn, a trip to Earth is a real experience. Furthermore, the friendly Earthlings will ensure you have a holiday to remember. As a result, places on the space-mobile are booked up quickly.

Be that as it may, many aliens are still reluctant to visit this lovely planet. But with new shuttle routes operating soon, this is set to change.

Test 7 Complex sentences
1 Zen fell asleep, falling into his cookie bowl.
2 After tidying her bedroom, Twinx had room to dance.
3 Pogo loves to bounce, even when he is tired.
4 Zing plays his music loud, enjoying the noise.
5 Nok grabbed his football, before racing out of the door.
6 Zara P checked her jet-scooter, preparing for a race.
7 The space-mobile took off, heading for Earth.
8 Twinx played with Mini T, despite having homework to do.
9 Pogo bounced in, leaving dirty spring marks all over the floor.
10 Looking carefully, you can see Dunk through a telescope.
11 The aliens won the competition, sending in the best entry.
12 Feeling excited, Zing pulled on his new trainers.
13 Zara P writes information in her notebook, so she can read it later.
14 Nok was man of the match, scoring the winning goal.
15 Running home in the rain, Twinx got soaked.

Test 8 Contracting sentences
1 The space-mobile is due to leave Dunk at 8.30am tomorrow.
2 Pogo's trainers have springs on them, which help him to bounce.
3 Zen finds it difficult to stay awake unless he eats lots of Z cookies.
4 Zara P can get about really quickly, because of her jet-scooter.
5 The planet the aliens live on is called Dunk and it is in another galaxy.
6 Zing downloads music onto his mp3 player so he can listen to it later.
7 Twinx loves Mini T, because she thinks Mini T looks just like her.
8 Pogo and Nok go to play football in the crater fields every Friday.
9 Zara P's notebook is full of information that she has written down.
10 Zen was snoring so loudly, you could hear it next door!
11 From Dunk, Earth looks just like a big blue and green football.
12 The stars around Dunk shine very brightly, especially at night.

Test 9 Writing balanced arguments
Answers will vary, but might include:
Space travel
1 It is very expensive.
2 It can be dangerous.
3 We might meet hostile life forms.
Girls playing football with boys
4 Boys can often run faster than girls.
5 Boys might play roughly and hurt the girls.
6 There is no need, because there are girls' football teams.
Having to do homework
7 It takes up too much of your free time.
8 You have to carry lots of books home.
9 If you get stuck, there is no teacher to help you.
Having a TV in your bedroom
10 It is lonely watching TV on your own.
11 If you stay up late watching TV you will be tired the next day.
12 It will stop you from reading.
Using public transport
13 You might have to wait for ages for a bus or train.
14 You cannot always travel exactly when you want to.
15 Journeys often take longer than by car.

13 Twinx's radio plays music so she can practise her ballet.
14 Nok scored three goals in his football match last Tuesday.
15 Pogo keeps Z cookies for Zen in his backpack.

Test 10 Conditionals
1 If I save up, I can buy a TV.
2 Going to the cinema would be really exciting.
3 We will be late if we do not hurry.
4 It will be too dark to see unless we put the light on.
5 Should Nok win the match, he will be over the moon.
6 If he is hungry, Zen loves eating Z cookies.
7 If he puts his trainers on, Pogo can bounce really high.
8 If Zing plays his music too loudly, people will be cross.
9 Assuming she remembers, Zara P is bringing home cakes for tea.
10 The comet may be visible from Earth soon.
11 Meeting new people can make Twinx feel shy.
12 Providing he gets his Z cookies, Zen will stay awake.
13 In a bouncing competition, Pogo could win first prize.
14 Twinx missed the space-mobile as a result of oversleeping.
15 Zen's team may win the trophy.

Test 11 Mnemonics

1	h	9	c
2	o	10	e
3	d	11	g
4	k	12	f
5	n	13	i
6	a	14	j
7	m	15	l
8	b		

Test 12 Biography and autobiography
Sentences 1, 2, 4, 7, 9, 10, 12, 14 are likely to come from an autobiography.

Sentences 3, 5, 6, 8, 11, 13, 15 are likely to come from a biography.

Test 13 Word origins

1	ski	Norwegian
2	umbrella	Italian
3	llama	American Indian
4	anorak	Eskimo
5	chocolate	Aztec, via Spanish
6	tattoo	Tahitian
7	circus	Greek
8	tornado	Spanish
9	tomato	Spanish
10	poncho	American Indian
11	bungalow	Hindi
12	café	French
13	castle	Latin
14	kiwi	Maori
15	wallaby	Australian aborigine

Test 14 Adapting text
Answers may vary, but the following is typical.
1 Find the ingredients.
2 Choose a large mixing bowl.
3 Ask an adult to pre-heat the oven to 180°C.
4 Ask an adult to take off the skin from a lemon with a sharp grater.
5 Ask an adult to slice the lemon in half.
6 Squeeze the juice from the lemon.
7 Throw away the lemon skin.
8 Mix the lemon zest, juice, sugar and butter.
9 Add 3 eggs, one at a time.
10 Stir quickly and without stopping.
11 Carefully stir in the flour.
12 Put the mixture into a cake tin.
13 Ask an adult to put the tin into the oven.
14 The cake should take 25 minutes to bake.
15 Let the cake cool down, then take it out of the tin.

Test 15 Checking your spelling
Circled words should be:

1	break	9	mobile
2	Swan	10	won
3	catch	11	radio
4	planet	12	space
5	rocket	13	bored
6	different	14	lost
7	great	15	brainy
8	about		

Test 16 Root words

1	light	9	clear
2	fold	10	mark
3	view	11	hand
4	move	12	rest
5	spite	13	build
6	fresh	14	vision
7	harm	15	love
8	play		

Test 17 Its and it's

1	It's	9	it's
2	it's	10	its
3	its	11	It's
4	it's	12	it's
5	its	13	its
6	it's	14	its
7	its	15	It's
8	its		

Test 18 Brackets
1 The space-mobile **(full of aliens)** headed for Earth.
2 Pogo's trainers **(with springs on)** were under his bed.
3 Earth **(seen through a telescope)** looks green and blue.
4 The meteor shower **(and astral winds)** continued all day.
5 Z cookies **(fed to him regularly)** keep Zen awake.
6 Twinx's hair ribbons **(all tangled up)** were in a pile on the floor.
7 Zara P put her notebook **(full of information)** in her bag.
8 Nok's football boots were filthy **(and soaking wet)**.

9 After lunch Nok and Pogo **(without his springy trainers)** played football.
10 Twinx's radio **(which she takes everywhere with her)** played music.
11 Zing sat **(looking cool)** by the crater.
12 Zen fell asleep **(as usual)** after tea.
13 Zing's music player **(which he bought on Earth)** is the latest model.
14 Zara P's jet-scooter **(at top speed)** gets her home in no time.
15 Pogo's rucksack **(stuffed with Z cookies)** was heavy.

Test 19 Formal official language
1 No parking.
2 No dogs allowed.
3 Not good for people to eat.
4 If there is a fire …
5 … please leave the building.
6 It is not the managers' fault …
7 … if your things get lost or broken.
8 Please keep your ticket …
9 … to get your money back.
10 Toilets …
11 … can be found around the building.
12 We will send your order …
13 … when you have paid.
14 If you lose your parking ticket …
15 … you will have to pay a release fee.

Test 20 Making new words

1	hydrocow	9	microshoes
2	macrobee	10	polyspotted
3	pyrotree	11	pyrobox
4	aquapig	12	cryptocode
5	hydrophone	13	subsnail
6	polytrunk	14	aquashield
7	cryptodoor	15	chromasoap
8	subcity		

Test 21 Unstressed vowels
Circled words should be:

1	parliament	9	separate
2	conference	10	easily
3	temperature	11	holiday
4	frightening	12	library
5	memorable	13	literature
6	generally	14	offering
7	deafening	15	interested
8	desperate		

Test 22 Personification
The knight's armour winked in the moonlight as he approached the castle. The drawbridge was lowered like a huge wooden tongue in the castle's great stone mouth. Its empty windows stared down at the knight from sleeping turrets. Ancient walls viewed the trespasser with hostility, while roosting birds muttered their disapproval.
The wind whispered around the crumbling walls, as the knight approached a crooked doorway crouched in a corner of the courtyard. It was framed by lanterns in which pale yellow flames danced.
Beyond the doorway, an old staircase stumbled its way crookedly upwards into the waiting darkness. Climbing, the knight's feet disturbed loose stones which chased each other back down the stairs, chattering as they went.
The castle had kept its secret for 100 years. Was it about to confide in this stranger?

Test 23 Adjectives

1	smallest	9	brighter
2	old	10	darkest
3	bigger	11	lazier
4	silliest	12	funny
5	warm	13	sadder
6	safest	14	latest
7	hungrier	15	tall
8	strange		

Test 24 Direct and reported speech
1 Zing said, 'My music is too quiet.'
2 'Could I have a Z cookie?' asked Zen.
3 'Where's Mini T?' asked Twinx.
4 Zara P said, 'I'm going out.'
5 Pogo said, 'I like bouncing.'
6 'I'm off to play football,' said Nok.
7 Zing asked Zara P, 'Have you seen Zen?'
8 'Zing, please will you fix my radio?' asked Twinx.
9 'Pogo, could you look in my notebook?' asked Zara P.
10 'I'm confused!' said Nok.
11 'The shop is closing,' announced the alien shopkeeper.
12 'I'm tired!' grumbled Zen.
13 'Let's go for a walk,' suggested Pogo.
14 'There are no spare seats,' said the space-mobile captain.
15 'Do you like my new trainers?' Zing asked Nok.

Test 25 Fact, fiction and opinion
Fact: 1, 2, 7, 8, 12

Fiction: 4, 5, 11, 13, 15

Opinion: 3, 6, 9, 10, 14

Test 26 Similes
Answers may vary, but well-known similes include:
1 as busy as a **bee**
2 as bold as **brass**
3 sleeping like a **baby**
4 run like the **wind**
5 as gentle as a **lamb**
6 swims like a **fish**
7 as light as a **feather**
8 pure like the driven **snow**
9 as white as a **sheet**
10 a face like **thunder**
11 as pretty as a **picture**
12 smoking like a **chimney**
13 as quiet as a **mouse**
14 eating like a **horse**
15 climbing like a **monkey**

Test 27 Genre
Science Fiction: 1, 5, 7, 10, 13

Westerns: 3, 6, 8, 9, 15

Historical Fiction: 2, 4, 11, 12, 14

Test 28 Visual clues for spelling
Correctly spelt words are:

1	successful	9	realistic
2	necessary	10	entrance
3	optimistic	11	fountain
4	transparent	12	hospital
5	boundary	13	magician
6	microscopic	14	magazine
7	transport	15	tropical
8	unbelievable		

Alien Club Certificate

Congratulations, _____, from everyone on planet Dunk!
You have collected all your award stickers and are now a member of the
English 10-11 Alien Club.
You are out of this world!